W9-BMU-298

My Friend Has ADHD

by Amanda Doering Tourville

illustrated by Kristin Sorra

Thanks to our advisers for their expertise, research, and advice:

Samuel H. Zinner, M.D., Associate Professor of Pediatrics
University of Washington, Seattle

Terry Flaherty, Ph.D., Professor of English
Minnesota State University, Mankato

PICTURE WINDOW BOOKS
a capstone imprint

Editor: Jill Kalz
Designer: Nathan Gassman
Production Specialist: Jane Klenk
The illustrations in this book were created with mixed media – digital.

Picture Window Books
151 Good Counsel Drive
P.O. Box 669
Mankato, MN 56002-0669
877-845-8392
www.capstonepub.com

Printed in the United States of America in North Mankato, Minnesota.
012011
006038VMI

Library of Congress Cataloging-in-Publication Data
Tourville, Amanda Doering, 1980–
My friend has ADHD / by Amanda Doering Tourville ; illustrated by
Kristin Sorra.
p. cm. — (Friends with disabilities)
Summary: "Explains some of the challenges and rewards of having a friend
with ADHD using everyday kid-friendly examples." — Publisher provided.
Includes index.
ISBN 978-1-4048-5749-0 (library binding)
ISBN 978-1-4048-6108-4 (paperback)
1. Attention-deficit hyperactivity disorder—Juvenile literature I. Sorra, Kristin,
ill. II. Title. III. Title: My friend has attention deficit hyperactivity disorder.
RJ506.H9T556 2010
618.92'8589—dc22   2009035269

My name is Marcus. This is my friend Robby. We've been friends forever. Robby has ADHD, which stands for attention-deficit/hyperactivity disorder.

Robby and I are on the basketball team at school.
Robby practices a lot. He helps me with my shooting.
He is one of the hardest-working players
on our team.

DID YOU KNOW? In the United States, about one out of every 25 kids has ADHD.

Robby and I love talking about sports. But sometimes he talks when he shouldn't. He isn't doing it on purpose. But I worry we'll get in trouble.

Shhh!

DID YOU KNOW? Kids with ADHD can be impatient. They might talk before thinking. They may blurt out an answer in class without being called on. They may interrupt a teacher or other students.

7

Robby has a hard time waiting his turn in the lunch line. We play quiet games like Rock, Paper, Scissors to pass the time.

Robby is always ready to try something new.

We've climbed a rock wall.

We've canoed.

10

We've even tried a zip-line!

DID YOU KNOW? Kids with ADHD are often open to new ideas.

Sometimes Robby says or does things that get him into trouble. He may get angry and start fights with other kids. I tell him fighting isn't cool.

DID YOU KNOW? Kids with ADHD don't always know how to act around others. They may cause arguments or fights, even when they don't mean to.

13

Robby has a hard time making friends. But once people get to know him, they really like him.

Robby's funny. He knows tons of good jokes.

15

I like working on school projects with Robby.
He's great at art and has awesome ideas.

DID YOU KNOW? Kids who have ADHD are often creative and have great imaginations.

17

After school, Robby and **I** study together. I share my books with him if he forgets his. We quiz each other until we know we can ace the test.

DID YOU KNOW? Kids with ADHD often forget to do things. They may also lose things easily.

19

Robby can't always follow directions very well.
He gets distracted. When we play games,
I make sure he understands the rules.

20

Then he
usually
beats me!

21

Being with Robby is never boring. He's always thinking of new stuff to do. Robby is a blast to be around. I'm glad he's my friend!

What Is ADHD?

ADHD stands for attention-deficit/hyperactivity disorder. ADHD is the most common behavior disorder in kids. Doctors aren't quite sure what causes it, but they think it may run in families. If one member in a family has ADHD, another member often does, too. Kids who have ADHD have trouble paying attention. They may daydream or "zone out" in class or at home. They may think about many things at once. These problems make it hard for kids with ADHD to concentrate. Kids with ADHD can have lots of energy and trouble sitting still. They aren't always able to control their behavior. They may say or do things without thinking. Doctors use medication and other kinds of therapy to help kids with ADHD stay calmer and focus better.

Glossary

concentrate—to focus tightly on just one thing

disorder—a kind of illness that affects the mind or body

distracted—having one's attention pulled from one thing to another

impatient—unable to wait quietly; restless

interrupt—to stop someone who is talking or doing something

therapy—treatment for an injury or physical or mental problem

To Learn More

More Books to Read

Kraus, Jeanne. *Cory Stories: A Kid's Book About Living with ADHD.* Washington, D.C.: Magination Press, 2005.

Nadeau, Kathleen G., and Ellen B. Dixon. *Learning to Slow Down and Pay Attention: A Book for Kids About ADHD.* Washington, D.C.: Magination Press, 2004.

Taylor, John F. *The Survival Guide for Kids with ADD or ADHD.* Minneapolis: Free Spirit Pub., 2006.

Internet Sites

FactHound offers a safe, fun way to find Internet sites related to this book. All of the sites on FactHound have been researched by our staff.

Here's all you do:

Visit *www.facthound.com*

FactHound will fetch the best sites for you!

Index

Look for all of the books in the Friends with Disabilities series:

My Friend Has ADHD

My Friend Has Autism

My Friend Has Down Syndrome

My Friend Has Dyslexia